Vol 8

MAZE

FOR KIDS

Ages 4-6

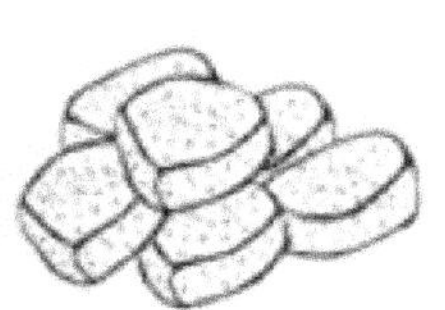

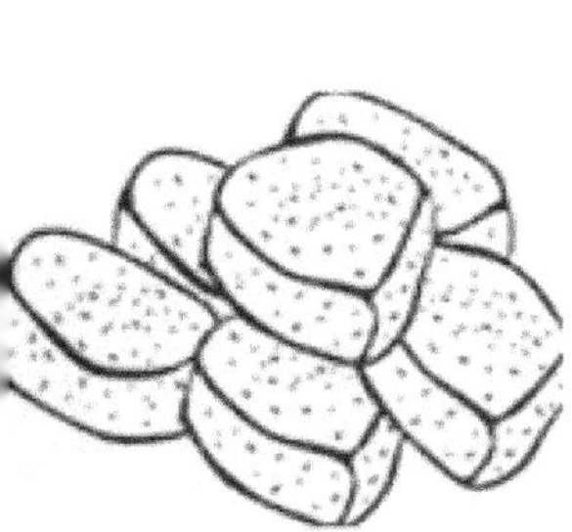

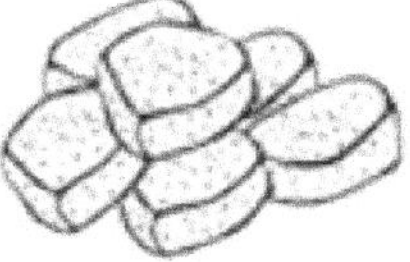

MAZE BOOK

SOCIAL MEDIA

- **f** /MySweetBooks1
- **🐦** /MySweetBooks1
- **📷** /MySweetBooks1
- **📌** /MySweetBooks

Email Us : mysweetbooks1@gmail.com

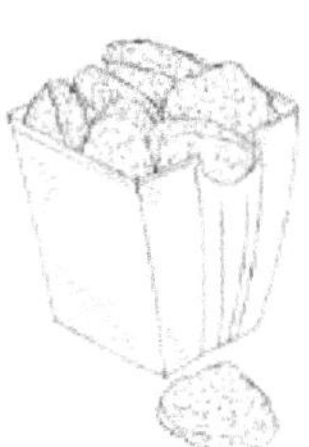

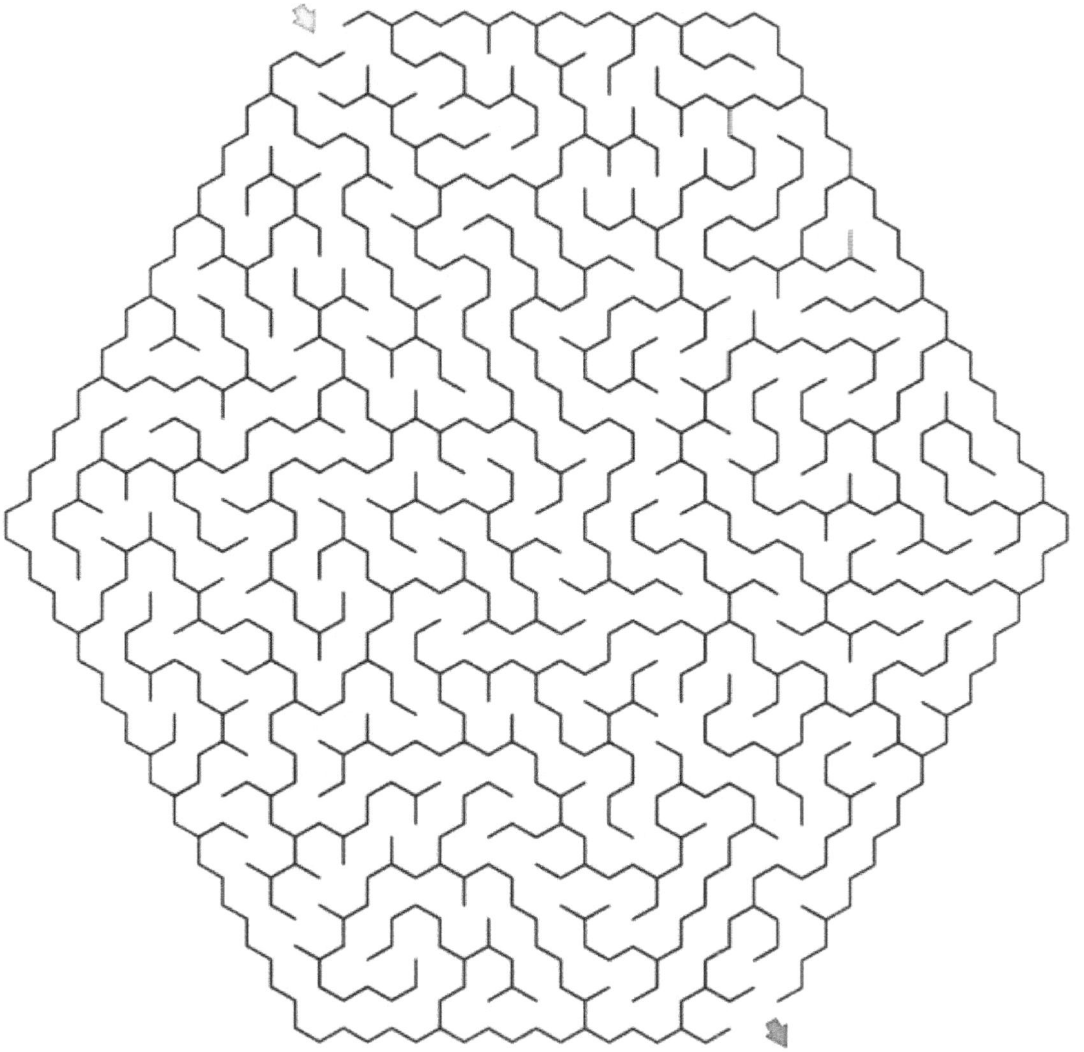

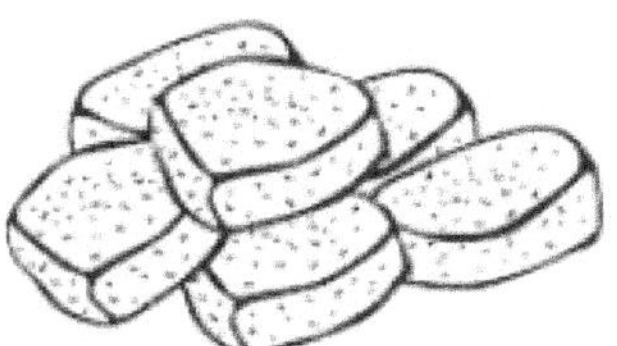

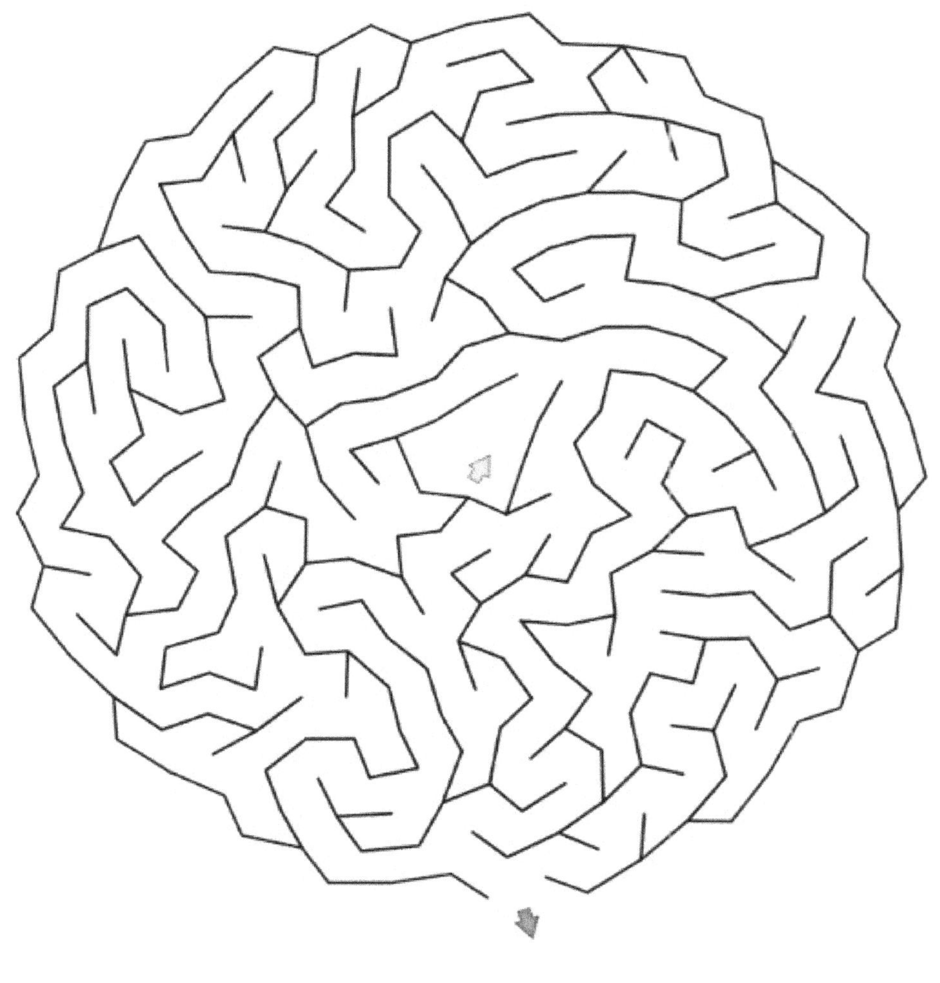

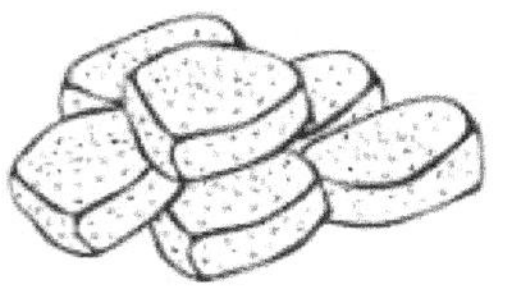

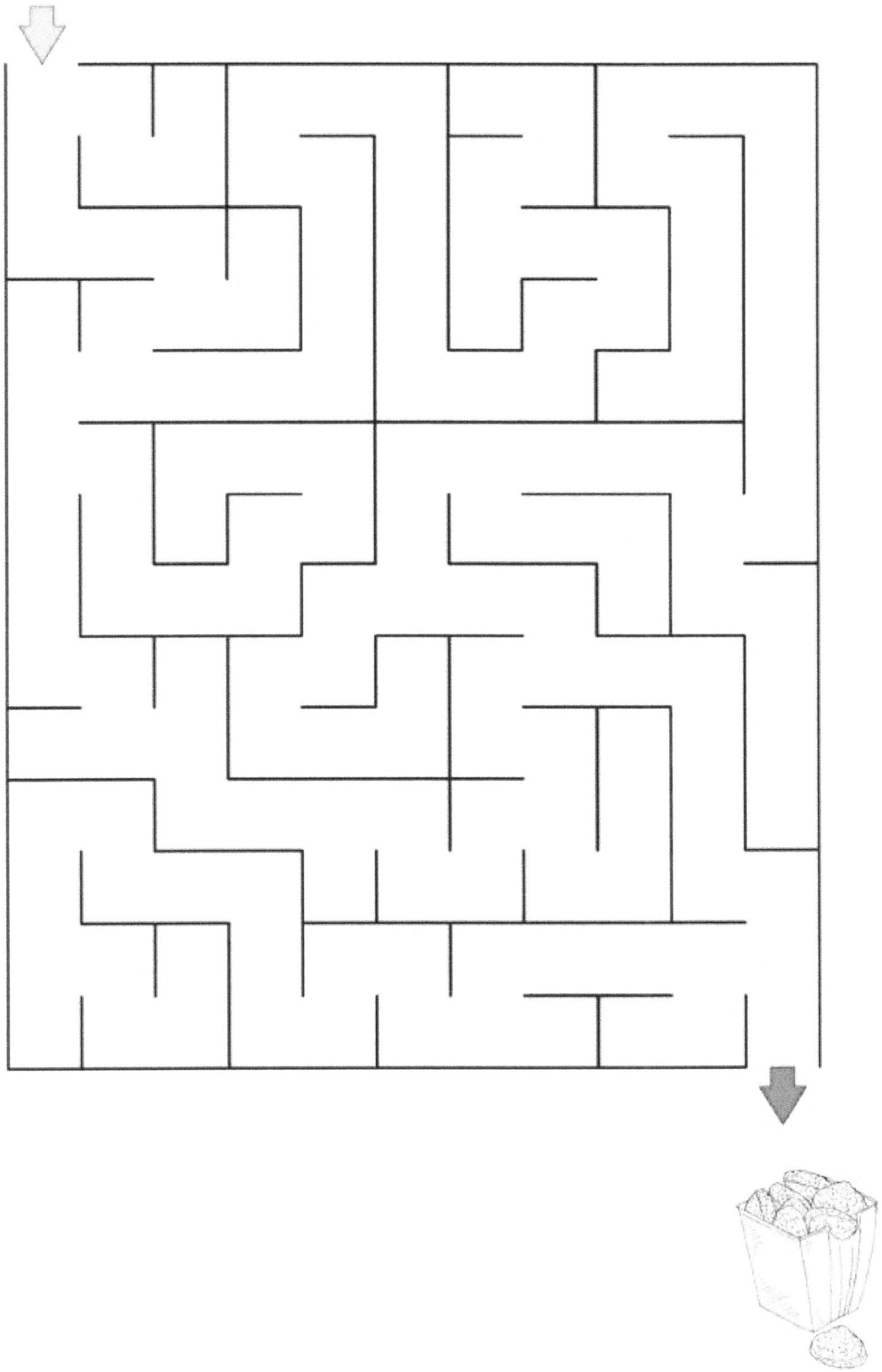

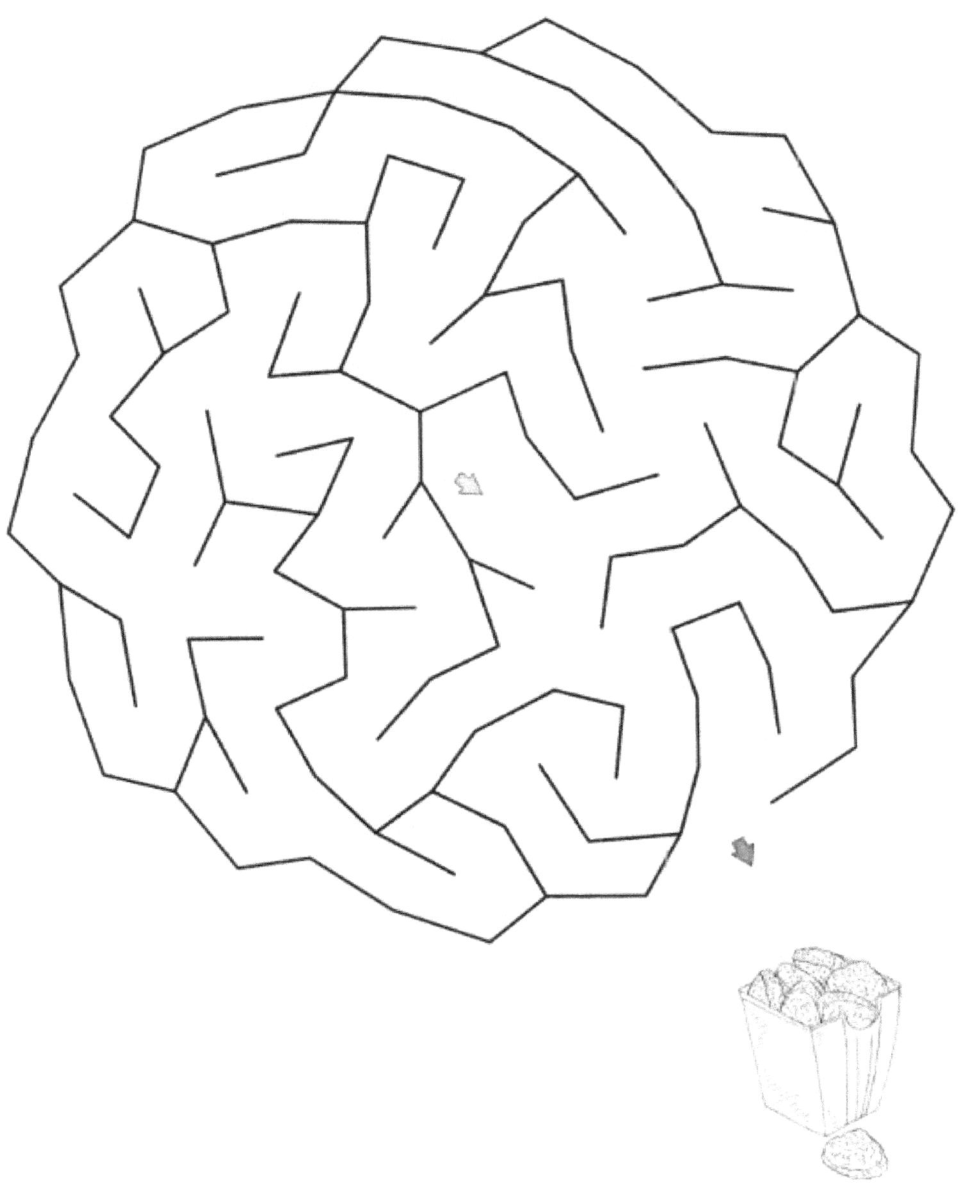

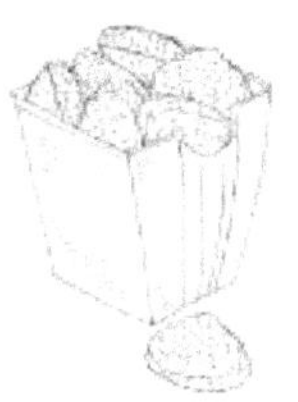

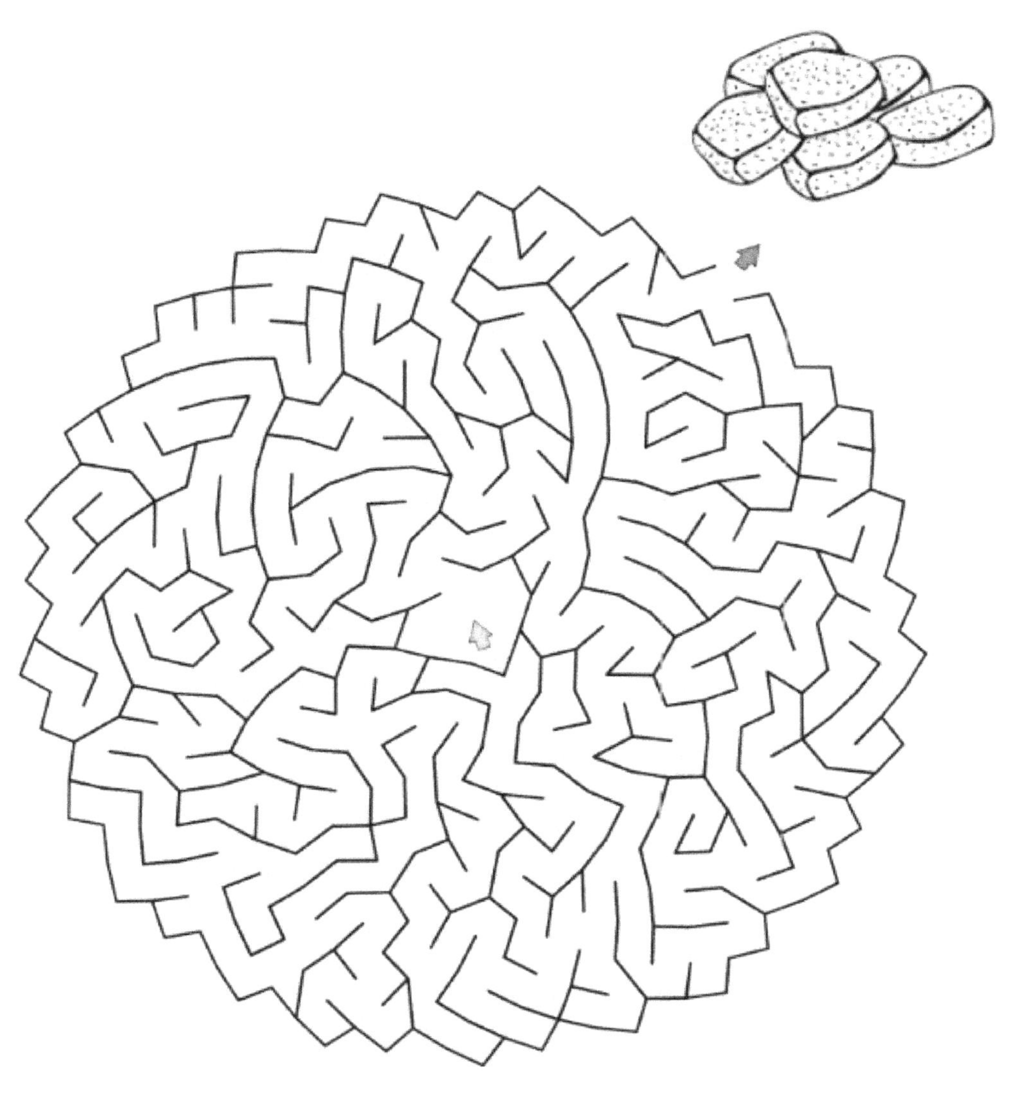

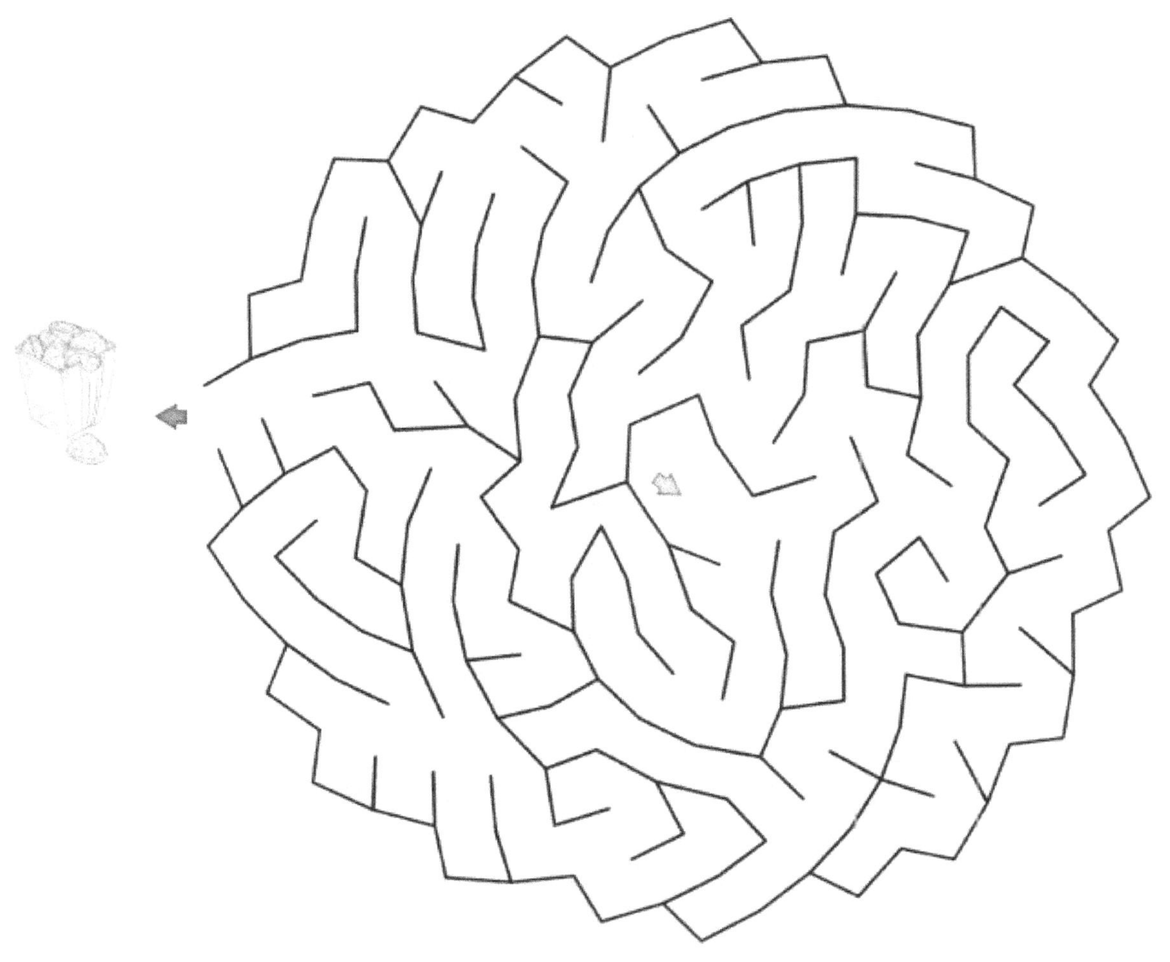

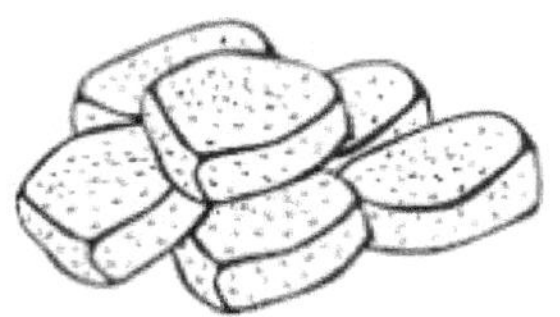

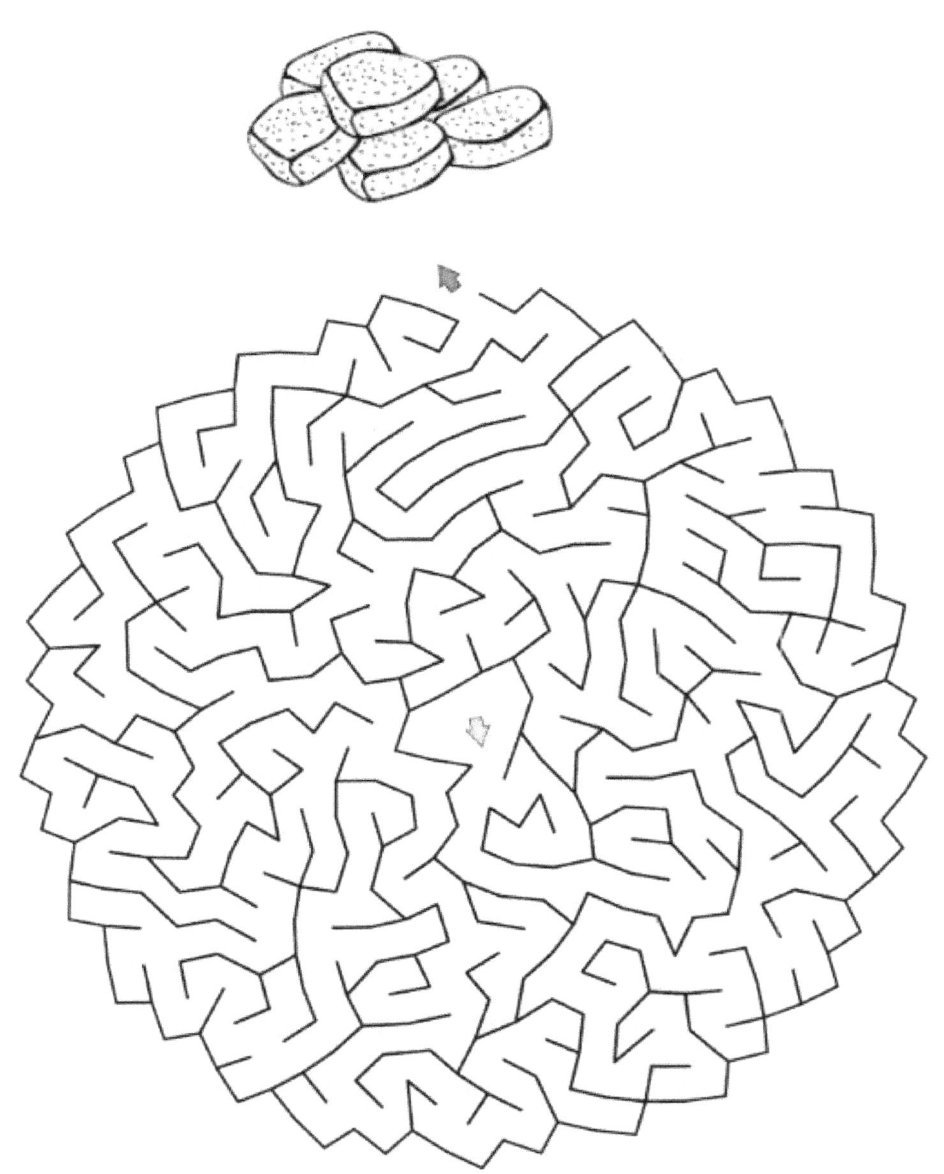